Poems

Hughes

POEMS.

BY

Mrs. HUGHES.

LONDON:

PRINTED FOR J. DODSLEY, IN PALL-MALL.

M.DCC.LXXXIV.

Work to you. The approbation of a
Lady, whofe tafte and judgment are
acknowledged by all who have the
honour of knowing her, affords me the
moft flattering profpect of its general
reception.

.I have the honour to be,

    M A D A M,

        Your Ladyfhip's

           much obliged

             and obedient

                humble fervant,

           A N N E   H U G H E S.

POEMS.

THE RIVALS.

A PASTORAL ECLOGUE.

DAMON, THIRSIS, AND DELIA.

NEAR the green margin of a filver flood,
    Penfive and fad, the love-lorn DAMON ftood;
Ah! wretched fwain! the haplefs fhepherd cry'd,
Ah! wretched fwain! again he faid, and figh'd;
To thwart my wifhes all things fure agree;
Like cruel DELIA, all things frown on me.
At early dawn of blithfome day I rofe,
With care my beft, my flender rod I chofe,
My fharpeft hook, and fineft line prepare,
And chufe my tempting baits with niceft care;

         The

The filver trout, all hope, I cry'd, fhall prove
A prefent pleafing to my cruel love :
But e'en the fimple finny race, of late,
Defpife my art, and fhun my tempting bait ;
This fingle trout, ah flender, worthlefs fpoil !
This fingle trout repays my lonely toil.
Ah ! wretched fwain ! the haplefs fhepherd cry'd,
Ah ! wretched fwain ! again he faid, and figh'd.

 Near the fame rivulet's green and fedgy fide
Young Thirsis rov'd, with love his theme and guide ;
There heedlefs oft the fhepherd wont to ftray,
And chant unfeen his foft, his love-tun'd lay ;
For Delia's heavenly charms alike poffefs'd
Each fhepherd's heart, and fir'd his faithful breaft :
Forlorn, abandon'd to his grief and pain,
He 'fpy'd the fad, the folitary fwain ;
Beneath a willow's weeping fhade he lay,
And caft his ufelefs rod with filent fcorn away.
With foft compaffion in his voice exprefs'd,
The gentle youth his love-lorn friend addrefs'd.

THIRSIS.

T H I R S I S.

Why mourns my DAMON ? why does he complain,
Yet leave his THIRSIS ftranger to his pain ?
What fad difquietudes can DAMON bear,
In which his friend is not allow'd to fhare ?
Why doft thou leave thy fheep at large to ftray ?
Why fcorn th' accuftom'd bufinefs.of the day ?
Why driv'ft thou not thy herds to yonder rill ?
Why doft thou fhun me on the neighbouring hill,
Where we were wont to tend our flocks at noon,
Obferve the evening clofe, and watch the rifing moon ?

D A M O N.

Can THIRSIS afk from whence my forrow flows ?
Too well, alas ! the cruel caufe he knows.
Haft thou not, falfe-one, by each method ftrove
To gain the fickle heart of her I love ?
Call me not friend, the falfe pretence I fcorn !
Friendfhip deceiv'd to deadlieft hate fhall turn !
Here let all amity, all concord end ;
Thy rival, I difdain the name of friend !

T H I R S I S.

Call me not falfe; by no infidious art
I've ftrove to gain the lovely DELIA's heart;
The fwain lives not who looks upon her eyes,
And does not wifh to win th' enchanting prize :
An equal right in the attempt I claim,
Unmafk'd my purpofe, and avow'd my flame;
With open love I woo the matchlefs fair,
Nor find much caufe for hope, nor yet defpair;
An equal fweetnefs in her fmiles I fee;
She fmiles on all, nor does fhe frown on me.

But fee, fhe comes; do thou the firft impart
The fecret forrows of thy love-fick heart :
Well doft thou know the fofteft art of fong,
For ftill the Mufe infpires thy tuneful tongue;
By gentleft numbers ftrive her heart to move,
For facred Poefy is the child of Love.

D A M O N.

Hail, cruel fair! bright caufe of all my woe,
From whom my every grief and pleafure flow.

Hail,

Hail, cruel fair! behold a haplefs fwain,

Who dares not hope, and yet muft breathe his pain.

Like plains imbrown'd by fierce meridian beams,

Uncool'd by zephyrs, unrefrefh'd by ftreams,

My bofom, parch'd by love's refiftlefs flames,

The fweet refrefhment of thy kindnefs claims :

But tho', like ftreams that murmur o'er the plain,

Thy charms delight the heart of every fwain ;

Tho' ftill on all you feem to fmile, you frown

On wretched DAMON, and on him alone.

THIRSIS.

Hail, charming maid ! in whofe refiftlefs eyes

Each artlefs, unaffected beauty lies ;

Thy gentle fmiles, with mirth and pleafure crown'd,

Diffufe a univerfal gladnefs round ;

Thy lively wit, bright child of Youth and Joy,

Soft as thy breaft, and piercing as thy eye,

Sweet theme of ev'ry Mufe, can ftill infpire

Cold age itfelf with rapture and defire :

With fmiles thy trueft votary regard ;

His bufinefs is to love, thy fmile his fweet reward.

B 3   D E L I A.

D E L I A.

Ceafe, fhepherds, ceafe; long have I known your love;
Neither I flight, yet neither can approve;
Your equal merits, equal praifes claim,
Alike your charms, your faith and love the fame;
And ftill upon the plain it is confefs'd,
In dance and fong you far exceed the reft.

   This hour fhall end the ftrife; the prize belong
To him who moft excels in gentle fong:
He who fings beft fhall beft his paffion prove,
For ftill the Mufes favour thofe that love.
Like ever-greens, in varying feafons gay,
My name fhall flourifh in your rural lay;
Deck'd by your praife fhall every charm improve,
Such glory waits the maid who wins a poet's love.
Straight then begin, your tuneful voices raife,
Myfelf the judge, reward, and fubject of your lays.

D A M O N.

How blithe was I, when, undifturb'd by love,
Thro' dale and woodland I was wont to rove;

Befide

Beside my flock to pass the live-long day,

Myself as chearful, and as mild as they;

Joyous my day, and peaceful was my night,

My flock my care, and friendship my delight;

With Thirsis did I climb the steepy hill,

Or wander'd thro' the wood, or by the rill;

No busy cares disturb'd my tranquil breast,

Light flew the hours, for Damon was at rest.

But since I saw thy eyes, alas! no more

I joy to greet the youth I lov'd before;

No faith or fellowship with him I hold,

Not more I hate the fox who thins my fold;

Silent and discontent I bend my way

To where yon aged oaks exclude the day;

Abandon'd and alone, to sooth my flame,

I call incessant on thy much-lov'd name,

I call, alas! but who regards my cries?

Sad Echo only to my plaint replies.

Too well I know 'tis fruitless to complain,

Too well I know my tears and sorrows vain,

But from the heart o'ercharg'd with pain and woe,

Unbid the sigh will swell, unbid the tear will flow.

THIRSIS

THIRSIS.

All day 't'as been my pleasing task to suit
The gentlest numbers to my warbling flute;
To chuse such sounds, as soft at once and clear,
Might steal like sweet inchantment on the ear;
Such magic numbers as might best impart
A glowing transport to th' enraptur'd heart:
For when sweet melody with poesy joins,
The soften'd heart each sterner thought resigns.
If in the soul a silent softness sleeps,
And, unperceiv'd, its secret station keeps,
Such numbers shall the sweet concealment break,
Give passion life, and teach it how to speak;
Such sounds the flame shall brighten and improve,
For music ever was the food of love.
My early study, and my latest care,
Is how to please, and most engage the fair;
And sure so soft, so delicate a mind,
To love so faithful will be just and kind.

DAMON.

D A M O N.

Behold my vagrant fheep at random ftray,

No crook to guide them on their deftin'd way,

No dog to keep; neglected and unfhorn,

Like their fad fhepherd, hopelefs and forlorn.

In vain the dance, in vain the fong invites ;

Nor dance nor fong my love-fick heart delights.

If it be love to fcorn all other joys,

To fhun my flock, to fpend whole days in fighs ;

If this be love, ah! then, alas! how well

This heart has lov'd, thefe heaving fighs can tell !

If it be love to languifh, to defpair,

To leave my hofe unty'd, uncomb'd my hair,

To doat with paffion on my woes and cares,

To fpend whole reftlefs anxious nights in tears ;

If this be love, ah! then, alas! how well

This heart has lov'd, thefe falling tears can tell !

T H I R S I S.

When on the plain the fprightly youth advance,

To chant the fong, and thread the mazy dance,

All

All undelighted I behold the throng,

Nor mingle in the dance, nor join the fong;

In vain I caſt my heavy eyes around,

No charm appears, no beauty can be found;

Too rude thofe rocks afcend, that vale's too low,

And clouds obfcure yon diftant mountain's brow;

The rofes fade, the violet hangs its head,

And, DELIA abfent, every charm is fled:

But fhould the miftrefs of my foul advance,

I join the fong, I mingle in the dance;

My nimble feet, refponfive to the found

Of fprightly pipe, fcarce feem to touch the ground;

Above the reft my chearful voice I raife,

By love and her infpir'd, to tune her praife;

The rocky fteeps again majeftic rife,

And the foft vale again inchants my eyes;

The diftant profpect brightens to the view,

And flowers that feem'd to droop, revive, and live anew.

D A M O N.

Oft have I known the fighs of the diftrefs'd,

With kindred fighs to agitate thy breaft.

When

When artful THIRSIS would thy ear affail
With the foft influence of a well-feign'd tale
Of two fond lovers, in whofe tender hearts
Cupid had fix'd a pair of pointed darts;
And how, for love of wealth, of fordid gold, .
The fair was to a richer lover fold;
Condemn'd, by cruel parents' harfh decree,
The youth fhe loves no more, alas! to fee;
How, torn afunder, fecret long they figh'd,
How for each other's fake at laft they dy'd;
And how, too late, the cruel parents mourn
Their age's comfort from their bofoms torn;
Oft have I feen thy foftly-heaving fighs,
And tears unbidden trickling from thy eyes.
Still, cruel fair-one, ftill doft thou incline
To bear a part in every woe but mine!

T H I R S I S.

When DELIA fings, 'tis extacy to hear
Her voice fo foft, fo foft, and yet fo clear!
Each fhepherd throws his pipe neglected by,
Delighted with her fweeter melody.

Enchanting

Enchanting maid! when I forget thy charms,

May foul diftortion fill thefe loathing arms :

Ere that, the woodlark fhall forfake the fhade,

And ere the rofe be blown, the bud fhall fade ;

The herd their wonted pafture fhall forego,

And at th' accuftom'd crib forget to low ;

The nightingale his plaintive fong give o'er,

And down yon rock the torrent ceafe to roar ;

In league the raven and the dove fhall join,

And the proud elm be lowlier than the vine.

D A M O N.

While the pale glow-worm glitter'd on the thorn,

And ere the lark proclaim'd th' approach of morn,

Thro' the drefs'd garden and the artlefs grove

I rang'd, to deck a garland for my love.

A wreath of various fweets did I compofe :

The painted violet, and the blufhing rofe ;

The columbine, that hangs her modeft head ;

The glowing pink, with ftreaks of various red ;

The pale jonquil, and fragrant jeffamine,

With ever-living myrtle did I twine.

Well pleas'd, the blooming prefent I prepare,

And hafte to bear it to the fweeter fair:

But while delighted o'er the plain I pafs'd,

The fun in radiance burft from forth the Eaft;

His heat grew ftrong: fpite of the hafte I made,

The rofes droop, the pinks the violets fade.

Near yonder lake with penfive fteps I drew,

And in, with fighs, the faded garland threw.

Still are we blefs'd when Fortune proves a friend;

But when fhe frowns, 'tis folly to contend:

E'en now, too fure, thofe partial eyes I fee

On THIRSIS fix'd, too fure averfe to me!

T H I R S I S.

As fate directed, or all-favouring love,

Near the fame fpot I penfive chanc'd to rove;

Mufing, around I caft my carelefs eye,

And on the lake the floating garland fpy:

A fhadowy cloud obfcur'd the folar beam,

The flowers bloom'd frefh upon the friendly ftream;

Joyful I bore the prefent to my fair,

And with it deck'd her fhining auburn hair;

Sweet

Sweet prefage of fuccefs ! fince which, imprefs'd
In livelieft tints, hope fills my glowing breaft;
And fure I read, in thofe dear, fpeaking eyes,
A fecret wifh that I may win the prize.

DELIA.

Ceafe, fhepherds, ceafe ! fufpend your tuneful lays ;
Your equal merits claim my equal praife :
To neither can the wifh'd-for prize belong,
For both alike excel in gentle fong.
But, DAMON, tho' a poet's praife be thine,
The palm of love to THIRSIS I confign.
Give o'er thy fighs, thy weak complaints forbear,
For know, the heart that loves can ne'er defpair;
Tho' doubts and fears the lover's peace moleft,
Hope ftill is nigh to chear his anxious breaft;
Whether in queft of pleafure or renown,
Hope ftill the beft, the beft thy hope fhall crown :
Courage alone can fortune's ills redrefs ;
He who deferves, will always hope fuccefs.
Seek then fome maid, in whofe accomplifh'd mind
Goodnefs with female elegance is join'd;

Leave

Leave every care behind thee, and to her,

With better hope, a happier fuit prefer:

So fhall thy honeft flame fuccefsful prove;

So fhall fhe meet thee with an equal love.

Ceafe then, fad youth, to languifh and complain;

Himfelf, not fortune, DAMON fhould arraign:

For ftill this ancient * maxim true fhall prove,

" He who defpairs, fhall ne'er fucceed in love."

* Faint heart never won fair lady.

ZARA;

ZARA; or, The SULTANESS.

AN EASTERN ECLOGUE.

THE vaſt ſeraglio blaz'd with radiant light,
 Gay ſounds of pleaſure charm'd the ear of night;
Rich brazen lamps adorn'd the ſtately rooms,
Glitt'ring with gems, exhaling ſweet perfumes:
Beneath the feet were ſplendid carpets ſpread,
And gilded roofs roſe vaulted o'er the head;
On golden hinges doors of ivory cloſe,
Embroider'd ſophas court to ſoft repoſe;
Voluptuous ſoftneſs ſunk in ſweet exceſs,
For Luxury had ſtrain'd her power to bleſs.
At SOLYMAN's command th' aſſembled fair,
To grace his hall and royal feaſt, appear:
Each charm was there that cauſe ſad lovers ſighs,
Soft roſy lips, blue veins, and ſparkling eyes;
The varied plume, the robes that looſely flow,
The beamy diamond, and the ruby's glow.

Around

Around the monarch caſt his piercing eyes;
And why is ZARA abſent? ſtern he cries;
Why comes ſhe not, a chief invited gueſt,
Why comes ſhe not to grace our royal feaſt?
Go, tell the haughty beauty—yet forbear;
Tell ZARA, SOLYMAN attends her here;
Tell her, her lord, deſcending from his ſtate,
An humble lover, on her ſmiles ſhall wait:
Yet bid her ceaſe her utmoſt power to prove,
Nor tempt too far our much-enduring love.
Thou, SELIMA, the ſullen fair invite
To ſhare the pleaſures of the feſtive night.

Swift as he ſpake, obedient to his word,
She flew to bear the mandate of her lord.
Far from her train retir'd the queen ſhe found,
To grief reſign'd, in hopeleſs ſorrows drown'd;
With ſoften'd voice, and ſweet beſeeching air,
She thus addreſs'd the melancholy fair:

S E L I M A

Why mourns the queen of SOLYMAN the Great?
What envious ſorrows tend her glorious ſtate?

What

What wifh ungratified can Zara know?

What blefling cannot Solyman beftow?

While fubject worlds own Solyman their lord,

Hang on his fmile, and live but by his word,

Uncharm'd by greatnefs, carelefs would he part

With fubject worlds, to reign in Zara's heart:

Not all the grandeur of his lofty throne,

His father's dazzling glories, and his own;

Not all the treafures of the golden Eaft;

Not the rich fplendours of the fumptuous feaft;

Not melting airs, that float the bowers among,

The mazy dance, the foft alluring fong;

Not yon bright circle of the gay and fair

Can charm our lord, if Zara be not there:

Yet fhe, retiring from his raptur'd eye,

Sheds the fad tear, and heaves the plaintive figh.

Bright Zara, to the royal feaft repair,

'Tis mighty Solyman attends thee there;

Thy lord, defcending from his wonted ftate,

An humble lover, on thy fmiles fhall wait:

But, ah! forbear thy utmoft power to prove,

Nor tempt too far his much-enduring love.

Z A R A.

Z A R A.

Curs'd be the hour that gave thefe haplefs charms
To hated SOLYMAN's detefted arms!
Oh! had I dy'd before that fatal day
Which tore me from my native plains away;
Then no proud tyrant had, with ftern controul,
Reftrain'd the inborn freedom of my foul,
Or vainly ftrove in fplendid chains to bind
Th' unbought affections, and excurfive mind.

No time the memory of my wrongs can chafe,
Back fhrinks my foul from his abhor'd embrace;
At his approach I hear Misfortune's moan,
His father * fhrieks, his captive brothers † groan:
No princely views his abject foul engage,
By turns he fhakes with pride, diftruft, and rage;
Then fpurns his trembling flaves, with power elate;
Cruel, yet foft; ftern, yet effeminate;

---

* Few of the eaftern princes die natural deaths, being generally depofed and murdered by their fons or fucceffors.

† When the Perfian monarchs mount the throne, they imprifon all their younger brothers for life; and, effectually to prevent their giving them any difturbance, put out their eyes.

The

The flowing robe, the fmile of ftudy'd art,

Conceal the harden'd, unrelenting heart.

Love flies the prifon where proud tyrants reign,

And fcorns the bafe involuntary chain !

Take back thefe dazzling gems, this gaudy veft,

And, oh ! reftore the peace of this fad breaft !

 Far from thofe paths which guilty greatnefs tread,

In deep retreat my infant days I led ;

An anxious mother nurs'd my tender youth,

And ftor'd my ductile mind with facred truth :

But, ah ! too foon, to dire difeafe a prey,

Death fnatch'd her kind, her gentle foul away.

Oh ! had I then, like her, to reft retir'd,

Dy'd at her fide, or in her arms expir'd !

Long did my eyes reject the dazzling light,

My ready foul was wing'd to take her flight,

When generous SELIM came to my relief,

Sooth'd my deep woe, and fhar'd in all my grief ;

His bofom heav'd with fympathetic fighs,

And focial tears flow'd plenteous from his eyes.

At length fair Comfort calm'd my troubled breaft,

And grateful Love my foften'd foul poffefs'd :

Our

Our parents mark our paſſion, and approve;
The morn was fix'd to crown our mutual love.

The fatal evening ſmil'd with calm deceit,
Soft breath'd the air, the choral ſong was ſweet.
Thus, ere the dreadful whirlwind burſts from far,
A death-like ſtillneſs calms the troubled air;
Thus Nature lulls the world in ſleep profound,
Ere the ſtrong earthquake rocks the ſolid ground.

O come my love, he cry'd, the roſes bloom,
The ſpicy groves emit a rich perfume;
The ſetting ſun declines his ardent beams,
Faintly they tremble in yon lucid ſtreams;
Nature revives to hail the parting day,
" Ariſe, my love! my fair-one, come away!"
Sweet was the gentle voice of him I love;
Smiling he led me to the ſpicy grove:
Behold, he cry'd, again yon radiant ſun
His daily circuit round the world has run;
Ere yonder radiant ſun again decline,
My lovely ZARA ſhall be ever mine.
Ardent he ſpake, to hope and love reſign'd,
Oh! blind to fate! to future anguiſh blind!

As

As near the foreft's inmoft maze we drew,

The troops of SOLYMAN appear'd in view:

The cruel fpoilers feiz'd me for their prize;

Vain were my lover's threats, his piercing cries.

Unhappy youth! thy anguifh ftill I fee,

Still flow thefe tears, ftill heave thefe fighs for thee!

But tho' they tear me from thy guardian arms,

Not force, nor bribes, nor flattery's foothing charms,

Nor time, nor cruel abfence, e'er fhall part

Thy much-lov'd image from my faithful heart.

Yes, cruel tyrant! tho' thy hated gate

Be clos'd with bars more ftrong than thofe of Fate;

Tho' fable eunuchs watch the hours of fleep,

And, open-ey'd, their ceafelefs vigils keep;

Tho' horrid mutes, with unmov'd ghaftly eye,

And fteady hand, the poifon'd bowl fupply;

Or quicker ftill, to foothe thy reftlefs hate,

The deadly bow-ftring end the work of fate;

Spite of thy caution, of thy jealous fear,

Pierce, pierce my heart! thy rival fhelters there.

Curs'd be the hour that gave thefe haplefs charms

To hated SOLYMAN's detefted arms!

Had we been born beneath the northern pole,

Where beauty faintly warms the languid foul;

Where the long frozen earth, and wintry fky,

Small means for art and luxury fupply;

Where love can little joy or anguifh give;

Where man's chief ftudy is the means to live;

Then, free from paffion, from affliction free,

Calm life had pafs'd in fair fecurity;

Tho' rapture's fweets our fouls could ne'er obtain,

Ne'er had they drain'd the bitter cup of pain.

Or rather, had fair Albion given us birth,

That feat of freedom, and that nurfe of worth;

Where varying feafons take their temperate turns,

Nor winter keenly bites, nor fummer burns;

No defert winds embrown her verdant plains,

No lawlefs fpoilers rob her labouring fwains;

No ftartled ear receives the captive's groan,

But Juftice guards, and Mercy gilds the throne;

Where generous Love and Reafon jointly reign,

And Senfe and Virtue rivet Beauty's chain;

Nor guards nor bolts their wavering faith fecure,

But Love, that form'd the vow, preferves it pure:

There

There had kind Heaven but fix'd our envy'd lot,

The humble tenants of fome peaceful cot,

Then wedded love had crown'd our conftant flame,

And fweet affection foften'd duty's claim ;

Kind confidence had blefs'd the focial day,

And peaceful years, unnumber'd, ftol'n away ;

Fair honour and efteem had crown'd my life,

And ZARA blefs'd the facred name of wife!

Ah ! charming dreams ! ye aggravate my woe,

Nor peace nor comfort fhall this bofom know.

 Curs'd be the hour that gave thefe haplefs charms

 To hated SOLYMAN's detefted arms !

No ray of hope, no tranfient gleam appears,

Thro' the dark vale of long fucceeding years ;

But frefh returns of fadly varied pain,

The lover's anguifh, and the captive's chain.

 There have been women who have nobly dy'd,

And feiz'd that freedom tyrants have deny'd ;

Why then endure this load of anxious cares ?

Why have not I a foul refolv'd as their's ?

Hence, idle fears ! hence to the timid breaft

By foft enfeebling happinefs poffefs'd !

Chafte

Chaste love shall gather courage from despair,

Arm my weak heart, and teach me how to dare!

Yes! wretched ZARA shall no longer sigh,

But seize her native privilege, to die!

   Go, tell thy haughty lord the vow I make,

Which prayers, nor threats, nor death itself, shall break:

    No future hour shall give these hapless charms

    To hated SOLYMAN's detested arms!

I see the ghastly mute before me stand,

The welcome potion in his pallid hand;

Eager I snatch the life-devouring bowl,

And drink sweet peace to this distracted soul:

But, ere I sink in everlasting rest,

My last deep sigh shall fly to SELIM's breast;

'Shall tell him, not the world's great Lord could part

    His much-lov'd image from my faithful heart.

THE

THE WANDERER.

A WINTER ECLOGUE.

TAKEN FROM A BEAUTIFUL EPISODE IN THOMSON'S
LAST SEASON.

'TWAS winter drear, all nature own'd its fway,
Brown were the fields, and leaflefs was the fpray;
The filent fongfter fhivering fought his neft,
The cattle droop'd, by fullen glooms opprefs'd;
Scarce could the ftruggling day its light obtain,
The cold dark night ufurp'd a lengthen'd reign;
The bleak north wind unceafing howl'd around,
And fleecy fnow conceal'd the frozen ground;
When from his tufted cottage hies the fwain,
To feek his flock on the extended plain.
With morn, flow rifing, was the fearch begun,
The tafk purfu'd till faintly fet the fun;
Then, fadly turning, back he fought to trace
His former fteps, with flow and weary pace.

5

Again the bleak north wind begins to blow,

Again defcends the foftly-falling fnow;

Chill evening clofes faft, in vapours loft,

All nature ftiffens in the bleaching froft.

Full many a labouring ftep he ftrives, in vain,

His former path, uncertain, to regain;

Nor land-mark can he fee, nor village fpire,

Nor fmoke far curling from the ruddy fire:

Amaz'd, perplex'd, unknowing where to go,

He gazes round, with looks of fpeechlefs woe;

With fudden fears and 'wildering doubts opprefs'd,

His hands he wrung, and fmote his heaving breaft;

And while each nerve confefs'd the fhivering fmart,

Thus burft the anguifh of his tortur'd heart:

Ah! whither fhall my wand'ring footfteps roam?

How find the path that leads me to my home?

A ftranger 'midft my native plains I ftand,

Unknown as diftant wilds, or tracklefs fand.

Her heavieft curtain night begins to fpread,

Nor know I where to turn, or fafely tread;

One level wafte the barren lands appear,

And earth and fky a kindred livery wear;

" Faft,

" Faſt, and more faſt, the flaky ſhower deſcends,"

No proſpect chears, no ſhelt'ring hut defends;

Thro' the thick air no ſtar emits its ray,

No beam appears to guide me on my way.

 Ah! whither ſhall my wand'ring footſteps roam?

 How find the path that leads me to my home?

What, if the cover'd pit my ſteps ſhould meet,

Or the freſh ſpring deceive my luckleſs feet?

The brawling brook, in icy fetters bound,

No longer warns me by its well-known ſound.

 What if, ſmooth'd up with lightly drifted ſnow,

I plunge where pointed rocks and brambles grow?

In vain my trembling limbs ſhall ſtrive to riſe,

Beneath their weight th' unſtable ſurface flies;

In vain I ſtruggle, numb'd and faint with fear,

No friend, alas! no ſaving hand is near!

In vain for aid my piercing cries reſound,

My piercing cries the howling ſtorm ſhall drown'd.

Where, where my flock, ill-fated, have ye ſtray'd?

What ſhapeleſs drift your dreary lodging made?

No more your hapleſs ſhepherd ſhall ye view,

Your ſhepherd, more forlorn, more loſt than you!

         Ah!

Ah! little think they, who, in ermin'd pride,

'Midſt idle ſtate and luxury abide,

Who on rich Perſia's labours ſoftly tread,

Or preſs in ſweet repoſe the downy bed;

Ah! little think th' effeminate and vain,

The flutt'ring tribes of ſummer's ſun-beam train, .

Who ſhun ſoft dews, and ſhiver at a breeze,

Ah! little think they of ſuch ills as theſe!

What words the anguiſh of my ſoul can tell!

My friends, my cot, my children, fare ye well!

And thou, my Lucy, at whoſe darling name

This boſom feels a laſt expiring flame,

Farewel, thou much-belov'd! oh! ceaſe to mourn

His abſence, who, alas! ſhall ne'er return!

Who now the means of comfort ſhall beſtow?

Who, who ſhall guard ye ſafe from want and woe?

In vain the wholeſome viands ye prepare,

Rouze the bright flame, and place the ready chair;

No more your ſmiles of love ſhall bleſs my ſight,

No more your artleſs ſongs deceive the night;

No more within theſe arms ye ſhall be preſs'd,

No more be folded to this guardian breaſt:

Scarce

Scarce can thefe ftiff'ning limbs fupport my frame,

This fault'ring tongue but half pronounce your name;

   No words the anguifh of my foul can tell:

   My cot, my wife, my children, fare ye well!

Defpairing fpake the fwain; when on his fight,

At diftance, brake a faintly glimmering light;

A fudden hope his icy heart poffefs'd,

A fudden warmth invades his freezing breaft:

As near the fpot, with quicken'd ftep, he drew,

His home, his much-lov'd home, appear'd in view;

Thro' the bright cafement fhone the ruddy flame,

A thrilling tranfport rufh'd thro' all his frame;

He fees his anxious Lucy watchful ftand,

His little ones with tears their fire demand:

Forward with extafy the Wanderer fprings,

No more complains of toil, nor longer envies kings.

V E R S E S,

VERSES,

WRITTEN UPON A SUMMER EVENING IN RETIREMENT.

MILD evening, not unwifh'd, returns;
 Her foft return will DAPHNE hail?
The fever'd air no longer burns,
 But frefhnefs breathes in ev'ry gale:
Nature puts on her fofteft form,
 Zephyr juft dimples the calm filver flood;
While plaintive Philomel's fweet note forlorn,
 Fills with mild melody the neighbouring wood.
Oh, come, dear maid! my flower-wove arbour grace,
With me invoke the facred Genius of the place.

Come, gentle Peace! daughter of Heaven, defcend!
 Thy fuppliant's ardent wifhes deign to crown;
Thou who art Virtue's ever-fmiling friend,
 Tho' round her dire misfortunes fternly frown;
          Oh!

Oh, Power benign ! thy footfteps let us trace
 O'er wooded upland, or by rivulet's fide ;
Oh ! condefcend our favourite haunts to grace,
 And in our focial cottage deign to 'bide :
For well we know, where Virtue dwells with thee,
Celeftial Happinefs muft love to be.

Be fweet retirement ftill our virtuous choice,
 Unlur'd by Folly's falfe, but dazzling blaze ;
Where Paffion liftens to calm Reafon's voice,
 And bright Reflection beams her facred rays ;
Where Charity appears with open hands,
 And foft Compaffion drops the tender tear ;
Where faithful Love the generous foul expands,
 And Friendfhip blazes, open and fincere ;
Where Honour ftrict the fteady bofom warms,
And Virtue fmiles ferene, in all her native charms.

Oh ! ye, by giddy Paffion led aftray,
 Hearken awhile to her perfuafive tongue ;
No thorn fhe ftrews in Pleafure's flow'ry way,
 But Peace attends her fteps, and Mufic tunes her fong.

I   With

With thy own fhield, bright goddefs, arm my breaft,

    Give me to chant thy praife the woods among;

Be friendfhip mine, and philofophic reft,

    Far from the crouded city's bufy throng :

For far from crouded haunts does Wifdom dwell;

She flies the bufy throng, and feeks the filent cell.

How little knows the diffipated breaft

    The pure and peaceful joys which thou canft give !

Little they know the fweets of rural reft

    Who in perpetual noife and guilty cities live ;

Where Avarice burns t' increafe his fordid ftore,

    Where Riot waftes what Penury fhould fhare ;

Where midnight broils oft bathe the fword in gore,

    And foul Difeafe infects the wholefome air ;

Where every crime and folly find a place,

And modeft Virtue hides her deeply blufhing face.

There dwell the fons of Softnefs and Excefs,

    Strangers to thee, and ftrangers to Delight ;

Who never knew th' angelic power to blefs :

    Languor confumes their morn, and Riot waftes

        their night.

There too the fair and thoughtlefs wafte their bloom,

 Unfocially polite, unpleas'dly gay;

Fantaftic joys their ill-priz'd hours confume,

 And fteal their ufelefs lives all unenjoy'd away:

Strangers to worth and dignity of mind,

Slaves of thofe little charms, to face and form confin'd.

Little they know the inexpreffive joy

 The friend fincere, the tender mother, feels;

The heart-felt fweets of Nature's magic tye,

 And the bright tear that from foft Pity fteals,

They never felt; they never knew the blifs

 That waits alone on happy focial life,

Never receiv'd the kind paternal kifs,

 Ne'er blefs'd the name of daughter or of wife:

Ah! how unlike what Nature meant to form,

With every virtue grac'd, complete in every charm!

Vainly, ye fons of Folly, ye pretend

 That Pleafure dwells in foftnefs and excefs;

To her fair 'bodes your fteps fhall never tend,

 Shall never reach the feat of heaven-born Happinefs.

Nor

Nor true delight that joyleſs wretch ſhall know,

   In whoſe cold breaſt the ſocial virtues pine;

His heart ſhall ſhrink with ſolitary woe,

   Tho' on his face eternal pleaſures ſhine:

For never joy ſhall warm the frigid breaſt,

Which, dead to ſocial love, is by itſelf poſſeſs'd.

Be ours far other wiſhes, other joys,

   Far other ſcenes be painted to our view;

Pleas'd will we 'ſcape from folly, glare, and noiſe,

   While reaſon bright, and fancy, ever new,

Our ſteps attend : we'll court the tuneful Muſe;

   The Muſe ſhall deign our fancy to inſpire,

The ſweeteſt ſtrains her influence ſhall infuſe,

   And fill our ſouls with her own ſacred fire;

To diſtant worlds tranſported ſhall they wing,

For what the Muſe inſpires, th'enraptur'd bard muſt ſing.

And thou, fair Peace, who lov'ſt the guiltleſs breaſt,

   Oh, come! and with thee bring thy radiant train,

Bright Confidence, Security, and Reſt,

   Exempt from Fear, Anxiety, and Pain;

        Oh,

Oh, come! our conftant foft companion be,

    Bring us Content and philofophic Eafe;

Humble Content; for, oh! if blefs'd with thee,

    The humbleft lot fhall fatisfy and pleafe:

For well we know, where Virtue dwells with thee,

Celeftial Happinefs muft love to be.

EPISTLE

EPISTLE

TO A

BELOVED SISTER,

WHO WAS ABSENT UPON A VERY LONG VISIT WITH
THE MUCH-ESTEEMED FRIENDS MENTIONED IN IT,
AND HAD SPENT SOME TIME AT H——— PREVIOUS
TO HER DEPARTURE.

FROM Moele's fair banks, whofe cryftal waters
    flow,
Since they forfook them, tun'd to murmuring woe;
From her cool bower thefe lines fad ANNA fends,
To greet, in diftant groves, her much-lov'd friends.
Health to my friends! where'er their fteps they bend,
May eafe and pleafure on thofe fteps attend.

Whether

Whether on Virniew's fragrant banks they ſtray,

Perfum'd with all the ſweets of new-mown hay;

Whether aſcend the hill, and thence ſurvey

The vale where Thanet ſteals its gentle way;

Whether the meadow's verdant boſom tread,

To ſeek the muſhroom in its graſſy bed,

Or through the varied garden chuſe to rove,

Or trace the mazes of the moſſy grove;

Whether, in queſt of Wiſdom's ſacred lore,

Th' hiſtoric or poetic page explore,

See doubts and errors by each ſearch remov'd,

Sweet feaſt of thought! improving and improv'd;

Or, tir'd with theſe, the frolic whim obey,

By Mirth inſpir'd, as innocent as gay;

Or Muſic ſoothe the ſoftly ſtealing hour,

Under the ſpreading tree, or fragrant bow'r;

Health to my friends! where'er their ſteps they bend,

May eaſe and pleaſure on thoſe ſteps attend.

But, ah! for me, my dear companions loſt,

What pleaſures can our late gay Hanwood boaſt?

'Twas not the fragrant garden's varied ſweets,

Its glowing beauties, or its cloſe retreats,

The

The murmuring brook, the cottage, or the grove,

Or facred name of home, that won my love

Like friendfhip: friendfhip gave them power to charm;

Friendfhip, benignly firm, and kindly warm.

Tho' a dear mother happily remains,

And my firft love, my tendereft duty claims,

Alas! what confolation can fhe be?

Silent fhe gazes round, and fighs like me.

Tho' either fifter claims an equal part,

An equal int'reft in her ANNA's heart,

Yet, abfent from her fight, for one fhe mourns,

And fondly counts the hours till fhe returns.

   Thus when fierce fever rages thro' the veins,

Or ague fhakes with life-confuming pains,

The tender mother views with fond defpair

Her dying hope, and makes him all her care:

In vain her rofe-lip'd cherubs round her throng,

To win th' accuftom'd fmile, with lifping tongue;

Each anxious thought on one dear care employ'd,

With hafty frown fhe chides them from her fide;

Neglects the happinefs fhe ftill can boaft,

And grieves inceffant for the bleffing loft.

When

When chearful morning, fresh from soft repose,

With all the charms of fragrant beauty glows;

When the sweet lark forsakes his lowly nest,

Upbraiding idle man's unneedful rest;

Like him refresh'd, the summons I obey,

And haste to hail the newly-risen day;

To the fresh garden's gilded shade repair,

But vainly seek my lov'd companion there;

Pensive the solitary walk prolong,

Or chearless tune my unattended song.

The little magic circle, that possess'd

The best affections of my faithful breast,

Disjoin'd and broken, cruel absence rends,

Deny'd at once to view my most-lov'd friends;

Deny'd in sacred amity to bind

Souls form'd for union, open and refin'd.

Fond, idle wish! in one fair hour to know

Those pleasures lengthen'd life can scarce bestow.

But, tho' remov'd from many a valu'd friend,

Her kindest amities the Muse would send;

Fain in her numbers would she see exprefs'd

The warmest dictates of her grateful breast;

To each lov'd abfent name fhe fain would pay
The grateful tribute of her fimple lay.

   Firft, for the mafter of that focial dome,
My gentle MARY's hofpitable home.
May varying bleffings crown the circling year,
May jocund Spring her greeneft mantle wear;
With rofes crown'd, gay Pleafure at her fide,
May Summer meet him in her glowing pride;
Never her ftores may niggard Ceres hoard,
But pour them plenteous on his ample board;
With wavy grain may golden harveft fmile,
And blefs with countlefs fheaves the reaper's toil;
The purple grape its richeft juice beftow,
The plum bloom fragrant, and the nect'rine glow:
And when cold Winter clofes up the year,
May attic mirth his focial dwelling chear;
Around his hearth may friend, fedately gay,
Steal the long evening unperceiv'd away.

   Nor be thou here forgot, dear, lovely maid!
O'er whofe young days pale Sicknefs cafts a fhade:
Yet chearful Patience can its fting difarm,
And rob fell Pain of half his power to harm.

Oh,

Oh, Health! thou life-endearing goddefs, hear!

To thee do I prefer my ardent pray'r!

To her pale cheek thy frefheft rofe fupply,

And light thy brighteft luftre in her eye;

With added charms her chearful life prolong,

And give her ANNA theme for future fong.

   What new regard expreffive fhall I fend

To thee, my dear companion! kindeft friend?

What ftrong expreffion fhall I find to prove

The ftronger feelings of a fifter's love?

But vain th' attempt, beyond the Mufe's art,

To fpeak the dictates of th' expanfive heart.

Never may danger, pain, or grief, intrude

On thy fweet hours of peaceful folitude!

Never may difcord, jealoufy, or ftrife,

Difturb thy happy days of focial life!

May all that can improve, exalt, refine,

May all that gilds, that fweetens life, be thine!

So fhall thy penfive ANNA ceafe to figh,

Catch thy gay fmiles, and fhare in all thy joy.

Sweet privilege of friendfhip! whofe rich ftore

Divided fwells, and, giving, gathers more.

                         Farewel!

Farewel ! and tho' the Mufe no genius fires,

Accept the tribute friendly love infpires :

Yet think not, tho' with cold, unpolifh'd art,

She feebly paints the feelings of my heart ;

Think not her carelefs, rude, and fimple ftrains,

Speak half the kindnefs which that heart contains.

A SONG,

A SONG,

FOR THE FAVOURITE WELCH AIR OF DAFYDD
GAREGWEN.

'TWAS on the Severn's fedgy margin
   Penfive DAFYDD chanc'd to ftray;
There, on the mofs-grown bank reclining,
   Tun'd to the winds his carelefs lay.

Steepy mountains heard his murm'ring,
   Echo caught the plaintive fong;
'Mong pendent rocks the wild notes warbling,
   Adown the dale foft founds prolong.

Sad his fate, whofe heart, ftill changing,
   Roves at large, and fix'd by none;
Happy he, who, free from ranging,
   Fondly loves, and loves but one.

WRITTEN

WRITTEN UPON THE DEATH

OF A

MOST SINCERE AND AMIABLE FRIEND.

INSTRUCT me, every friendly power,
    Inftruct me to complain,
To tell, in dear MARIA's death
    The lofs that I fuftain:
Yet little need I to invoke
    The aid of ftudy'd art;
From grief fincere fpontaneous flow
    The feelings of the heart.

This heart thy lofs fhall ever feel,
    Thy lofs fhall ever moan;
For, ah! with thee, from this fad breaft
    What happinefs is flown!

Thy

Thy converfe fweet, dear, much-lov'd maid !

  Could every care remove ;

'Twas pure as friendfhip's holy vow,

  Soft as the fmile of love.

With thee the fummer day was fhort,

  Nor winter evening tir'd,

Whether with fweet reflection fraught,

  Or fprightly wit infpir'd.

Ah me ! how light are Pleafure's wings !

  How fwift fhe fleets away !

A day of forrow is an age,

  An age of joy, a day.

Ah ! why did Heaven our fouls unite,

  So foon condemn'd to part ?

Ah ! why, fince form'd for fo much pain,

  Beftow the feeling heart ?

Yet, Senfibility ! to thee

  We every pleafure owe ;

The heart that never felt thy pains,

  Shall never tranfport know.

Not

Not always Virtue's radiant fhield
 Her favourite breaft defends,
Not always on the guilty head
 The threaten'd ftroke defcends;
Elfe had not innocence and worth
 Felt Pain's invenom'd dart;
Elfe had not Death, with ruthlefs fting,
 Pierc'd dear MARIA's heart.

Yet let me not, too rafh, complain
 Of all indulgent Heaven,
Who knows when fitteft to refume
 The bleffings it hath given.
Had Fortune, juft to thy deferts,
 With high exalting hand,
Plac'd thee in fcepter'd grandeur great,
 To blefs fome diftant land;

Unenvying had I view'd thy ftate,
 Had feen thee fhine above the reft,
And, tho' condemn'd to lofe my friend,
 Rejoic'd that fhe was blefs'd.

And

And haſt thou not a brighter crown,
 A more exalted throne,
Than eaſtern monarchs can beſtow,
 Or low ambition known ?

Then let me ſtudy to deſerve
 In bliſs like thine a part,
To meet thee in the realms of love,
 And ſhare again thy heart.
Hence, ſelfiſh grief! to joy ſublime
 Hope every pang refines;
So o'er the dark deſcending cloud
 The glitt'ring rainbow ſhines.

WRITTEN UPON A VERY HOT MORNING IN JULY.

WHEN the bright fun has reach'd his middle day,
And downward darts his fierce meridian ray;
When panting herds take fhelter in the wood,
Or plunge impatient 'midft the foaming flood;
When filent fongfters feek the bower's retreat,
When Nature faints, opprefs'd by fervent heat;
Give me, ye Powers, unfeen, at large to rove
Thro' the thick mazes of the fragrant grove;
On the cool moffy bank to court repofe,
Or watch the murm'ring rivulet as it flows;
Well pleas'd to view on its tranfparent breaft
Calm Nature's faireft image foft imprefs'd,
And, mufing on its glaffy furface, fpy
The fhadowy clouds that in its bofom fly;
Feel the cool zephyr wing'd with frefhnefs blow,
And diftant view the fhower-portending bow;

E   Then

Then fee the glofly rain defcend apace,

Dimpling the filver current's polifh'd face;

Attend reviving Nature's chearful voice,

Receive the flow'rs perfume, and hear the birds rejoice.

Far higher pleafure fhall my foul receive,

Than joylefs crowds or cumb'rous pomp can give;

From each low paffion fhall my heart be free,

Refin'd by Nature's fweet fociety.

Bright when fhe blooms in ev'ry opening flower,

Breathes in the gale, refrefhes in the fhower,

Oh! fay with what a foul he is endu'd,

Who vacant gazes round, and calls it folitude?

To DOCTOR ———,

WHEN A STUDENT AT EDINBURGH.

WRITTEN UPON THE FOURTH OF JULY,

BEING HIS BIRTH-DAY.

UNSKILL'D in foft poetic ftrains,
   No Mufe affifts, no Genius fires;
Yet kindly will a friend receive
   The tribute true efteem infpires;
The wifh fincere, that every good
   His future days may ceafelefs blefs,
From every ill his fteps fecure,
   And, as his years increafe, increafe his happinefs.

May pleafure ever on thy fteps attend,
   And, wing'd with joy, each moment fleet away!
Free from each felfifh paffion be thy breaft,
   Clear as the heavens, and as the feafon gay :

E 2

Not

Not pleasure, such as agitates the heart,

A rough, disturb'd, and overwhelming flood;

But pure, unmix'd, congenial to the soul,

The heaven-delighting power of doing good.

How little knows the vot'ry of excess

The joy serene that from compassion flows!

He who ne'er knew th' angelic power to bless,

Ne'er felt the purest bliss that Heaven on man bestows:

To pour cool freshness thro' the fever'd veins,

To rob fierce torture of its keenest smart,

To raise from paleness the enliv'ning bloom,

Light the dim eye, and ease the throbbing heart;

To wipe sad tears from the paternal eye,

To bid reviving hope illume the breast;

Or, where the healing art can nought supply,

By gentle acts to comfort the distress'd;

From deeds like these, which angels might partake,

. Far higher pleasure shall thy soul receive

Than low Ambition ever could bestow,

Or laughing Folly to her votaries give.

Such

Such deeds be thine; and may approving Heaven
 In recompence each real good beftow,
Give thee to tafte of every pure delight
 Which from benevolence and kindnefs flow:
So fhall each year of added life
 A thoufand heart-felt bleffings bring;
So every good and every blifs be thine,
 Which from th' untainted fource of fteady virtue
  fpring.

Thus, as the year's revolving round
 Brings chearful on thy natal day,
With pureft pleafures be it crown'd,
 And, wing'd with joy, purfue its circling way.

EDWIN

EDWIN AND MATILDA.

A LEGENDARY TALE.

IN THREE PARTS.

IN ancient days, when Britain's fons
    Were govern'd by the fword,
Ere equal laws alike had bound
    The peafant and the lord;

In caftles fenc'd with moat and wall
    Two haughty barons reign'd,
And ftill, with unabated hate,
    A deadly feud maintain'd.

Nor lefs their vaffals, ftern and bold,
    With fettled rancour burn;
While mutual injuries provoke
    A quick and fure return.

Each

Each hour fome caufe of deep offence
 Their kindling fury found;
Whence wild confufion, ftrife, and death,
 Embroil'd the country round.

E'en to the chace in arms they went,
 To guard precarious life;
And oft the friendly feaft became
 A fcene of deadly ftrife.

SEWARD, to MORKER's Earl allied,
 Rode out at early morn,
To trace the woodland foreft wild,
 With hound and bugle horn.

Juft at the entrance of the plain
 Young HENRY's train appear,
Prepar'd, on courfers fleet and fair,
 To hunt the flying deer.

At once their ire began to glow,
 At once they gave command
To check their courfers ardent fpeed,
 And made a mutual ftand.

     Then

Then gallant HENRY, young and brave,
    Fix'd his firm fpear in reft,
And fpurr'd his fiery courfer full
    Againft bold SEWARD's breaft.

But fix'd as ftands the fea-wafh'd bafe
    Of fome time-rooted rock,
The warrior firm retains his feat,
    And fcorns the threat'ning fhock.

At once their breathlefs fteeds they quit,
    And fpring upon the plain;
There, face to face, and hand to hand,
    The combat to maintain.

Quick forth their fhining faulchions fly,
    With mutual rage they burn;
Like lightning flafh their glitt'ring blades,
    And wound for wound return.

Sufpenfe poffefs'd the anxious mind
    Of every gazing knight;
Nor knew they what to hope or fear,
    So equal feem'd the fight.

                    Young

Young HENRY, active, light, and warm,
  With thirst of glory fir'd;
And SEWARD, cautious, cool, and firm,
  By deadly hate infpir'd.

Long hung the fight with dubious poife
  In doubt's uncertain fcale;
Nor either combatant gives way,
  Nor either can prevail:

Till SEWARD, rouzing all his might,
  With ftrength refiftlefs prefs'd,
And plung'd his keen and fatal fword
  In youthful HENRY's breaft.

So falls the oak or lofty pine,
  When furious ftorms prevail;
So finks the high-erected tower,
  When lightnings fierce affail.

To arms! to arms! fierce ELDRED cried;
  Oh! let it ne'er be faid,
That unprotected, unreveng'd,
  Our gallant leader bled!

His

His honour'd corfe fhall they refign
 Ere we from fight retire;
That mournful prefent will we bear
 To his afflicted fire.

To arms! to arms! each knight exclaims;
 Oh! let it ne'er be faid,
That unprotected, unreveng'd,
 Our gallant leader bled!

Nor lefs bold SEWARD and his train
 For hardy deeds prepare;
Furious they burn to meet the foe;
 Their fhouts refound in air:

But foon, by force fuperior prefs'd,
 The prize of glory yield;
And flow retreating, ftep by ftep,
 Indignant quit the field.

Brave HENRY's corfe his friends obtain,
 And fadly flow retire,
The mournful off'ring to prefent
 To his afflicted fire.

          Ah!

Ah! who fhall paint the father's grief
　　(The painful tafk I fhun)
When breathlefs, pierc'd with many a wound,
　　He faw his only fon?

Ah! who fhall paint the cruel pangs
　　That rent his manly breaft,
When in his arms, convuls'd with woe,
　　The lifelefs youth he prefs'd?

But foon, fuperior to complaint,
　　His grief to fury turns;
Ardent he grafps his trufty fpear,
　　His foul for vengeance burns.

Arm! arm! my valiant friends, he cries,
　　Due vengeance to obtain;
Earl MORKER fhall not live to boaft
　　The hour my fon was flain!

E'en to his heart will I repay
　　My valiant HENRY's death;
To-morrow fhall the ftrife begin,
　　Nor end but with his breath.

Hie

Hie to the loftieſt battlement,
    There ſound the bugle horn;
Bid all my vaſſals arm'd attend
    Before the riſing morn.

Arm! arm! my valiant friends, he cries,
    Due vengeance to obtain;
Earl MORKER ſhall not live to boaſt
    The hour my ſon was ſlain!

––––––––––––

PART THE SECOND.

THE bugle horn, with ſhrilleſt blaſt,
    Pierc'd thro' the ſtill night air;
The vaſſals hear the well-known ſound,
    And to their chief repair.

Arm'd with the faulchion, ſpear, and bow,
    Obedient to the call,
Ere morning dawn, with ready haſte,
    They crowd his ample hall.

                      There,

There, on a bier with fable hung,
   The lifelefs youth they view;
Thus, ere the Earl his woes could fpeak,
   Their fatal fource they knew.

With horror ftruck, and ftrong furprize,
   Some ftart with wild amaze;
While others droop the forrowing head,
   Or ftand in filent gaze.

In deepeft grief their chieftain ftands;
   His unmov'd, mournful eyes
Fix'd on the melancholy bier
   Where his lov'd HENRY lies.

At length his head he flowly rais'd,
   And view'd the duteous band;
Then thrice in vain effay'd to fpeak,
   And thrice he wav'd his hand:

' Too much of weak, unmanly tears
   ' Already have been fhed;
' 'Tis time, my friends, with other rites
   ' We grace th' illuftrious dead.

                                ' 'Tis

' 'Tis not by soft complaints and sighs
 ' The brave should speak their woe;
' For every tear the hero sheds
 ' A tide of blood should flow!

' Behold your youthful leader slain!
 ' His blood bold SEWARD stain'd;
' But deeply shall he rue the hour
 ' Such fatal fame he gain'd.

' Rouse, rouse your wonted force and might!
 ' Oh! let it ne'er be said
' In MORKER's hall, that unreveng'd
 ' Your youthful leader bled!'

He spake, while every list'ning ear
 Hung eager on the sound;
He ceas'd, and instant murmurs rose
 The vaulted hall around.

Lead us, with ardent voice they cry,
 Sure vengeance to obtain;
Earl MORKER shall not boast the day
 Our gallant chief was slain!

That

That hour their silent march begun,
 Ere fled the drowsy night;
And with the morn Earl MORKER's towers
 Salute their eager sight.

From off the loftiest battlement
 Aloud the watchman cried,
Arm! arm! Earl GODWIN's followers pour
 Down the steep mountain's side.

The welcome found bold MORKER hears,
 And from his soft couch springs;
With vows, and threats, and clashing arms,
 The lofty castle rings.

Around their chief crowds many a knight,
 Of faith and valour tried;
And with the first young EDWIN came
 To guard his father's side.

His manly form in fairest mould
 Was cast, with every grace;
Proportion'd strength his limbs adorn'd,
 And faultless was his face.

In

In nature's prime, when manly years
    Juſt ſhade the brow of youth ;
When glory fires the ardent ſoul,
    And love of ſacred truth.

His radiant eyes diſplay'd a ſoul
    Awaken'd and refin'd ;
Each look and changing feature ſpoke
    A pure and perfeƈt mind.

Arm'd in a coat of ſhining mail
    The youthful hero ſtands,
And, fir'd with glorious thirſt of fame,
    The promis'd fight demands.

Nor long the promis'd fight delays ;
    All eager to obtain
Bright viƈtory, the hoſtile bands
    Soon meet upon the plain :

There, front to front, in order'd ranks
    They ſtand, a martial ſight !
Impatient till the trumpet's ſound
    Gives ſignal for the fight.

The

The trumpet gave the wifh'd-for found;
    Each chief, with fpear in reft,
Like lightning fpur'd his rapid fteed
    Againft his rival's breaft.

But who fhall fpeak the hardy deeds
    Of every valiant knight ?
Deeds whofe high prowefs well might claim
    A Homer to recite.

Ill fuited to the female pen
    Are war's uncouth alarms,
The rattling car, the neighing fteed,
    And dreadful din of arms ;

Then moft delighted, to defcribe
    Sweet fcenes of rural joy,
When Peace her downy wings unfolds,
    And war and difcord fly.

Ere ceas'd the lark's firft mattin lay
    The furious fight begun,
Nor ended till the weftern fea
    Receiv'd the fetting fun.

                                Ah!

Ah! then how dreadful 'twas to view
   Honour's enfanguin'd bed,
With trampling fteeds, and arms difpers'd,
   The dying, and the dead!

In every form of horror drefs'd,
   Grim Death at once appears;
A thoufand ftern and ghaftly fhapes
   At once the monfter wears.

Among the flain bold MORKER lies,
   With deathlefs glory crown'd;
And near his fide young EDWIN, faint
   With many a deep-felt wound.

Each manly fear the hero wore
   Right on his duteous breaft,
Nor ceas'd his hand to grafp the fword,
   Tho' fhades his eyes opprefs'd.

Full oft in vain bold SEWARD ftrove
   The battle to renew,
Nor quits the fanguinary field
   'Till night obfcures his view:

He quits the field; but in his foul
   Revenge and hatred burn,
And many an ardent vow he breathes
   Of quick and fure return.

Triumphant GODWIN now remains
   Sole mafter of the field,
And vaunts aloud, that every power
   To his, perforce, muft yield.

Around he views the deathful fcene,
   And gives command, to bear
The wounded knights from off the field
   With kind and courteous care.

With courteous care the wounded knights
   They to his hall convey;
But leave the dead, in proud contempt,
   To ravening wolves a prey.

To dungeons, dark and comfortlefs,
   The prifoners are confign'd;
But youthful EDWIN in a ftrong
   And lofty tower confin'd.

We

We pafs young HENRY's obfequies;
    The ceremonial ftate
Was fuch as wont upon the great
    And titled lords to wait :

Which paft, and folemn mourning o'er,
    Earl GODWIN gives command,
That EDWIN and the prifoner knights
    Before his eyes fhould ftand.

His hall, with many a warrior bold,
    And beauteous dame, was grac'd ;
And near his fide his lateft hope,
    The fair MATILDA, plac'd.

Not morning opening to the view,
    Which light and warmth fupplies,
A foften'd luftre could difplay
    To emulate her eyes :

In all the glow of youthful charms
    She fhone beyond compare ;
By many an humble knight confefs'd
    The faireft of the fair.

                        With

With fix'd regard, on EDWIN's face
   Fierce GODWIN turn'd his eyes;
His HENRY's form, his HENRY's years,
   Fresh grief and rage supplies:

Yet calm his aspect he preserves,
   Nor did his eyes impart
The settled hatred and revenge
   That rankled at his heart.

Thus ever-varying sweets exhale
   From Ætna's verdant fields,
Each spicy grove and flow'ry vale
   Exhaustless beauty yields;

But while all distantly admire
   Her sides in richness dress'd,
Eternal bursts of raging fire
   Feed on her tortur'd breast.

Far different were young EDWIN's thoughts,
   By different objects fir'd;
MATILDA's face had caught his eyes—
   He wonder'd, and admir'd.

So

So fair a face, fo fair a form,

His eyes had ne'er beheld,

So much in every charm and grace

The lovely maid excel'd.

Long, in delight and rapture loft,

His eyes had feafted there,

But foon the pleafing charm was broke

By GODWIN's voice fevere :

' Behold,' he cries, with waving hand,

' Behold the certain woes,

' The fure captivity and fhame

' That tends on GODWIN's foes !

' Valour and fortune both unite,

' In this aufpicious hour,

' To throw the ftrength of MORKER's houfe

' Entirely in my power.

' Before my unrefifted might

' This band reluctant bends,

' For well they know upon my will

' Their future fate depends.

' But

' But think not that, on vengeance bent,

  ' We're not to mercy prone ;

' For still to conquer and forgive

  ' In noble minds is one.

' By mercy sway'd, unhop'd, unsought,

  ' This hour it is decreed,

' That, without suit or ransom paid,

  ' Each valiant knight be freed :

' One sacrifice, and one alone,

  ' Justice, severe, demands ;

' One victim HENRY's ghost expects

  ' From these avenging hands.

' As in the curs'd and bloody fray

  ' My sole support was lost,

' No youthful heir for ever shall

  ' The house of MORKER boast.

' To-morrow, ere Aurora bright

  ' From out the east has pass'd,

' E'en on the spot where HENRY fell

  ' Shall EDWIN breathe his last.'

  A shriek,

A fhriek, as of extreme diftrefs,
   Refounded through the hall;
The prifoner knights before the Earl,
   Imploring mercy, fall.

Not EDWIN fo; with mind ferene
   He heard his fentence pafs'd,
And on his unrelenting foe
   A look fuperior caft.

' Think not I fear to meet my fate,'
   With fteady voice he cry'd,
' Yet would that in the fields of fight,
   ' Like MORKER, I had dy'd!

' That from fome brave and equal hand
   ' My foul had freedom found,
' Rather than from her feat expel'd
   ' By bafe plebeian wound.

' Yet not on me difhonour refts;
   ' The brave can never fhare
' That infamy, contempt, and hate,
   ' Cowards and tyrants bear.

                    ' Thy

‘ Thy offer’d mercy I would fcorn ;

   ‘ Nor would I wifh to live

‘ For any prize, fave one alone,

   ‘ Within thy power to give.

‘ Nor can thy pride and ruthlefs hate

   ‘ A pang fo keen prepare,

‘ That EDWIN boafts not fortitude,

   ‘ Without a groan, to bear.’

Then on MATILDA’s lovely form

   Again he fix’d his eyes,

But fees her face bedew’d with tears,

   Her bofom heave with fighs ;

On fair ELTRUDA’s faithful breaft

   Reclin’d her penfive head :

For him he knew thofe fighs were heav’d,

   For him thofe tears were fhed.

Then, falling at her father’s feet,

   She rais’d her fuppliant eyes,

And feiz’d, with eager grafp, his hand,

   And thus with ardour cries:

                       ‘ Forgive

‘ Forgive thy kneeling daughter's tears,

  ‘ Nor let them flow in vain,

‘ But let her from thy oft-prov'd love

  ‘ Her pleaded fuit obtain!

‘ Oft, when thy foul hath been poffefs'd

  ‘ By dire revenge and hate,

‘ Oft haft thou heard MATILDA's voice,

  ‘ And ftopp'd the arm of fate:

‘ Once more, oh ! let her prayer prevail!

  ‘ Let not Misfortune fhare

‘ Thofe bafe and painful punifhments,

  ‘ Which only Guilt fhould bear!

‘ Nor Juftice, tho' fevere and ftern,

  ‘ Such facrifice demands;

‘ Nor HENRY's ghoft fuch deed expects

  ‘ From thy avenging hands:

‘ From earthly drofs and paffions free,

  ‘ His foul no more fhall know

‘ Our wretched ftate, or aught regard

  ‘ That paffes here below.

        ‘ Then,

' Then, great in arms, in power complete,

   ' Oh ! let my father's name

' With deeds of heaven-born mercy fill

   ' The filver trump of Fame !

' For fweeter is the heart-felt praife

   ' Which generous acts obtain,

' Than the harfh found of conquefts won,

   ' Or thoufand rivals flain.'

She ceas'd; for in her father's eyes

   The gathering furies burn,

While thus he frames his quick reply,

   In accents harfh and ftern :

' Stop, bold prefumer on my love !

   ' Stop, ere my anger glows,

' Ere I account my only child

   ' Amongft my deadlieft foes !

' Such fhall I reckon every one

   ' Who would divert my hate,

' Or ftrive to fnatch fierce MORKER's fon

   ' From his impending fate.

                              ' Hence,

' Hence—dry thofe weak and idle tears,'
   He faid, with anger fir'd:
Slow from his feet the fair-one rofe,
   And, fighing deep, retir'd.

What then were youthful EDWIN's thoughts,
   By fudden hope poffefs'd?
Then Love triumphant feiz'd at once
   The empire of his breaft.

At parting fuch a look fhe gave,
   Shot thro' a pearly tear,
'Twas more than pity could infpire,
   More ardent, more fincere.

Ah! magic fweet of youthful love,
   That with fuch eafe can rear
The tender plant of blooming hope,
   'Midft barren, cold defpair!

By gentle Pity's voice unfway'd,
   Stern GODWIN gives command,
That ere the dawn his vaffals, arm'd,
   Before his gate fhould ftand;

Le

Left any, by compaſſion mov'd,
  To Seward ſhould diſcloſe
The ſecret of young Edwin's fate,
  And he the deed oppoſe.

PART THE THIRD.

NOW evening, with her duſky wings,
  Obſcur'd the face of day,
And ſunk in deep oblivious reſt
  The ſilent caſtle lay.

All but Matilda's gentle eyes
  Were clos'd in downy ſleep;
Thoſe eyes which, ſince ſhe left the hall,
  Had never ceas'd to weep.

' And muſt he die!' ſhe faintly cry'd,
  ' In life's too pleaſing prime!
' Die by the hands of violence,
  ' Tho' free from ev'ry crime!

' Far

'Far other fate, if babbling Fame
   'Report his actions right,
'Far other fate from Fortune's hand
   'Deserves the youthful knight.

'And sure, if well I read his eyes,
   'Within his manly breast
'Each generous virtue is contain'd,
   'For all are there exprefs'd :

'Nay more, if rightly I conceive,
   'They told me, were he free
'To spend his life as choice would lead,
   'That life he'd spend with me.

'And shall I tamely sit and weep,
   'Of saving power poffefs'd,
'While the fell murderer's ruthlefs sword
   'Is plung'd in EDWIN's breast ?

'Ah, no! that power will I exert
   'Ere it be yet too late,
'Nor wafte in doubt a fingle thought,
   'But fnatch him from his fate.'

                A faithful

A faithful fquire the fair-one had,
　　Obedient to her will,
Who wont her bounties to beftow,
　　And generous acts fulfil;

For other fecret, till that hour,
　　MATILDA never knew:
Him to her fight fhe calls, and quick
　　Inftructs him what to do.

A liquid fhe poffefs'd, whofe power
　　With influence foft would fteep
The tafter's fenfes, long and fure,
　　In deep unconfcious fleep:

This fhe commands her faithful fquire
　　To take with inftant hafte,
And in a bowl of wine infufe,
　　Which every guard muft tafte.

Next, in the habit of a page
　　Her beauteous form fhe drefs'd;
And, while compaffion urg'd her fpeed,
　　And fill'd her gen'rous breaft,

　　　　　　　　　　　　　　Nor

Nor fear, nor virgin diffidence,
 Her ardent fteps reftrain;
And danger threats, and duty calls,
 And reafon pleads in vain.

With feet that lightly prefs the ground
 She reach'd the lofty tower,
Where EDWIN, firm and undifmay'd,
 Expects his fatal hour.

Upon her ear a gentle voice
 In plaintive numbers ftole;
She lift'ning ftood, while EDWIN pours
 The feelings of his foul.

' Yes, lovely maid!' he fondly cries,
 ' Contented will I die,
' Since for my fate that gentle breaft
 ' Will heave a pitying figh.

' Still in my ear thy accents found,
 ' Thy lifted hands I fee:
' Did fhe not kneel, and plead, and weep?
 ' MATILDA wept for me!

2   ' Ye

' Ye balmy fighs, ye precious tears,

  ' Once more for EDWIN flow!

' And, oh! be this the only grief

  ' That gentle breaft fhall know!

' Thy image from my faithful heart

  ' Not torture fhall remove;

' Nor till that heart forgets to beat.

  ' Shall it forget to love!'

No longer durft the liftening maid

  Indulge her wifh to hear;

For now the moon was mounted high,

  The midnight hour was near.

' Up, up, fir knight, with fpeed!' fhe cry'd,

  ' My leading fteps attend;

' In me behold a faithful guide,

  ' And a determin'd friend.

' No time for queftion now remains,

  ' For inftant flight prepare;

' Thy devious fteps will I direct,

  ' And every danger fhare.'

     G   ' Ah!

' Ah ! fure thofe accents well I know,'
  The eager lover cries;
' Too deeply on this heart imprefs'd
  ' Are thofe angelic eyes !'

' Forbear,' replies the blufhing maid,
  ' Nor wafte the fwift-wing'd hour;
' On inftant flight thy life depends;
  ' Fly while 'tis in thy pow'r !'

' And wilt thou ! wilt thou,' cries the youth,
  And feiz'd her trembling hand,
' Thy EDWIN's fortunes deign to fhare,
  ' His future life command ?'

With fault'ring voice the fair replies,
  ' In vain would I conceal
' The fentiments that fway my heart,
  ' Which looks and deeds reveal.

' MATILDA's future hours of blifs,
  ' In number and degree,
' Her future days of joy or woe,
  ' Muft all depend on thee.

                              ' Hafte

' Hafte then! the moments fly apace,
   ' Too long our fteps delay !'
She faid: they from the tower defcend;
   Her fquire directs the way.

Clofe by the fleeping guards they pafs;
   Aided by powerful love,
Before them bolts and bars give way,
   All obftacles remove.

Clear fhone the moon's refplendent orb
   With bright and favouring ray;
The ftars with fparkling luftre glow'd,
   To light them on their way.

While many a tender tale he tells,
   On EDWIN's arm reclin'd,
With hafty fteps the fair-one leaves
   Her native walls behind.

Juft as the fun's firft trembling beam
   Difpel'd the fhades of night,
His ftately caftle's lofty towers
   Salute glad EDWIN's fight.

 Before

Before them ran the trufty fquire,
  And to the watchman calls;
Tell gallant SEWARD that your Earl
  Approaches near thefe walls.

The guards repeat the welcome found,
  The found bold SEWARD hears,
But fcarcely dares indulge his hopes,
  Or check his ftronger fears;

Till from the battlement again
  He hears the watchman call,
And inftant burfts of mingled joy
  Re-echo thro' the hall.

Around their lord his vaffals prefs,
  Enraptur'd at his fight;
Nor lefs the joy brave SEWARD feels,
  And every faithful knight.

' Welcome,' they cry, ' our much‑lov'd lord,
  ' In every danger try'd;
' Thou lateft prop of MORKER's houfe,
  ' Its fole fupport and pride!'

Well

Well pleas'd, he marks their duteous zeal;
  But wills them to confer
All honours on his lovely guide,
  All homage pay to her.

Next he the venerable prieft,
  Without delay, commands,
In holy wedlock's facred bonds
  To join their plighted hands;

Then bade with dance and feftive mirth
  The happy day be crown'd:
He fpake, with founds of general joy
  The vaulted roofs refound.

From off the loftieft battlement,
  Aloud the watchman cry'd;
Arm! arm! Earl GODWIN's followers pour
  Down the fteep mountain's fide.

Arm! arm! each valiant knight exclaims,
  And meet the vengeful foe;
In EDWIN's and MATILDA's caufe
  Our blood fhall freely flow!

G 3   All

All pale, upon her EDWIN's breaſt
   Reclin'd the trembling fair ;
' Ah ! ſpare,' ſhe cry'd, ' MATILDA's life,
   ' Her aged father ſpare !

' What guilt, alas ! could equal mine,
   ' What miſery could exceed,
' If by my huſband's ruthleſs ſword
   ' My wretched ſire ſhould bleed ?'

' Diſmiſs thy fears,' he fondly cries,
   And claſp'd her to his breaſt ;
' Oh ! never be, by EDWIN's fault,
   ' This gentle heart oppreſs'd !

' Thy ſire ſhall be my conſtant care,
   ' Throughout this hated ſtrife,
' Sacred to me as late I held
   ' The noble MORKER's life.'

' One dear requeſt I ſtill would make,'
   Replies the generous fair ;
' Oh ! let me on thy ſteps attend,
   ' And every danger ſhare.

                        ' When

‘ When wounded, fhall my ready hand
  ‘ The healing balm apply;
‘ So will I fave thy precious life,
  ‘ Or on thy bofom die.’

‘ Let better hope illume thy mind,’
  With foften’d voice he cries;
‘ But, oh! forbear, forbear to afk
  ‘ What love itfelf denies!

‘ Each future happinefs of life
  ‘ With thee I’ll freely fhare;
‘ But every danger, toil, and pain,
  ‘ Myfelf alone would bear.

‘ Then fare thee well, thou moft belov’d!
  ‘ My abfence ceafe to mourn:
‘ Heaven, for my fweet MATILDA’s fake,
  ‘ Will fpeed my fwift return.’

He fpake, and, breaking from her arms,
  Quick join’d his martial train;
Who, burning ardent for the fight,
  Soon reach the hoftile plain.

Nor

Nor lefs the ardour of the foe;
 Infpir'd by vengeful hate,
Where'er fierce GODWIN lifts his fword,
 He deals the blows of Fate.

With ruthlefs ire around the field
 He hunts for EDWIN's life,
Who cautioufly eludes his fearch,
 And flies the dreaded ftrife.

No other can his might withftand;
 Where'er the warrior turns,
Terror and flight precede his fteps,
 And dire confufion burns.

At diftance, loud fierce GODWIN cries,
 ' Turn, bafe and recreant knight!
' No longer fly this lifted arm,
 ' Turn here, and prove its might!'

So fwift the thundering warrior prefs'd
 On his reluctant foe,
Scarce had he time to mark his aim,
 Or fhun th' impending blow.

        Then

Then down he dropp'd his ufelefs fpear,

 And bar'd his manly breaft;

And thus, with fupplicating voice,

 His haughty foe addrefs'd:

' This happy morn thy daughter dear

 ' Became my wedded wife;

' Forbid it, Heaven, a fon fhould dare

 ' To feek a father's life!

' Ah! rather on this duteous knee

 ' Thus let me fue for peace;

' Let all paft enmity and hate

 ' Betwixt our houfes ceafe!

' But if fubmiffion nought avail

 ' Thy fettled hate to move,

' Strike here, and pierce the faithful heart

 ' That boafts MATILDA's love.'

United hate and fury burn

 In rancourous GODWIN's eyes;

' Yes, take the death thou haft deferv'd!'

 With quivering lip he cries:

' My

' My ruin'd houfe, my children loft,
  ' This great revenge demand !'
He fpake, and lifts the pond'rous fword
  High in his blood-ftain'd hand.

With lightning's fpeed, unfeen before,
  Forward MATILDA prefs'd;
And while fhe cried, ' Spare, fpare my love ! '
  Receiv'd it in her breaft.

' Thrice welcome wound !' the fair exclaims;
  ' Without complaint or figh,
' To guard from harm her much-lov'd lord
  ' Shall glad MATILDA die !

' Thy fafety was my only care,
  ' 'Twas all that I defir'd !'
Then, faintly fmiling, prefs'd his hand,
  And in his arms expir'd.

Amaz'd, he feels her bofom cold,
  Beholds her eye-lids clofe,
And on her cheek the lily pale
  Succeed the blufhing rofe.

Diftraction feiz'd his trembling frame;
     ' Return, return!' he cried;
Then, bending fenfelefs o'er her form,
     His quivering accents died.

But, foon reviv'd to keener pangs,
     Her clay-cold lips he prefs'd,
And heav'd an agonizing figh,
     And ftrain'd her to his breaft.

' Oh! ftay, MATILDA, ftay!' he cried,
     ' Our loves not death fhall part!'
Then feiz'd his fword with fatal fpeed,
     And plung'd it in his heart.

PASTORAL

PASTORAL BALLADS.

PASTORAL THE FIRST.

WHY fighs my lov'd DELIA fo deep?
  Why flies fhe the fight of her fwain?
In fafety thy lambkins may fleep,
  The wolf is chas'd far from the plain.
See the meadows in verdure are drefs'd,
  Thro' the corn-waving vallies we'll rove;
Come, tell me the pains of thy breaft,
  Thofe pains let thy THIRSIS remove.

Tho' DAPHNE has wedded a fwain
  Whofe riches are greater than mine,
Tho' vanity fwells in her train,
  And luxury bends at her fhrine;

Of worlds were thy fhepherd poffefs'd,
   Thofe worlds he would freely impart;
He has made thee the queen of his breaft,
   And thy charms are enthron'd in his heart.

Has Delia forgot when we ftray'd
   Thro' the coppice that grows by the mill,
While the nightingale fung in the fhade,
   And the willows hung over the rill?
How fhe vow'd that her fwain and her cot
   Were the all of her humble defire,
That fhe envy'd no princefs her lot,
   Or to pleafures more high would afpire?

When we watch'd the clear rivulet glide,
   Regal'd by the fweet-fcented hay,
Fair Chearfulnefs fmil'd by my fide,
   And Content tun'd the nightingale's lay:
Thy fmile could charm forrow away,
   Could paffion and anguifh controul;
Thy fmile was the beam of my day,
   And the funfhine that gilded my foul.

                     Ah!

Ah! why does ambition intrude,

   Our exquifite blifs to deftroy,

To poifon the fweetnefs of life,

   And dry up the fountain of joy?

Ambition let heroes purfue,

   Quitting peace for its buftle and glare;

But what has ambition to do

   With the gentle, the kind, and the fair?

Since DELIA no more can delight

   To ramble the woodlands among,

Where the hawthorn blooms gay to the fight,

   And the thrufh tunes his elegant fong;

No more in thofe woodlands I'll ftray,

   No more in yon valley I'll rove;

For it was not the nightingale's lay

   That made me fo fond of the grove.

Thofe founds which fuch joy could impart,

   Now increafe both my anguifh and moan;

No pleafure can chear my fad heart

   When I range thro' the woodlands alone.

                           But

But come, my lov'd DELIA, oh! hafte;

   To charm thee all nature unites:

Each innocent joy let us tafte;

   It is love, 'tis thy THIRSIS invites.

On my arm thou fhalt gently recline,

   Sweet converfe fhall fhorten the hour;

The magic of love fhall refine,

   And add fweets to each gale and each flower:

The thrufh, as delighted we ftray,

   His elegant fong fhall repeat;

The valley again fhall be gay,

   And the nightingale's lay fhall be fweet.

PASTORAL

PASTORAL THE SECOND.

WHY flies the fleet chariot fo fwift,
 That conveys my falfe lover away ?—
Ah, cruel ! reflect on thy vows !
 Stay, barbarous CELADON, ftay !
Reflect on thy vows and thy fighs,
 How oft thou haft fworn to be true :—
See ! fwifter and fwifter it flies ;
 Ah me ! it is loft to my view !

Ye virgins, fo artlefs and gay,
 Be timely admonifh'd by me ;
Nor ever attend to the vows
 Of a youth of fuperior degree.
When they tell you their love is fincere,
 Ah ! truft not the flattering guile ;
Regard not the figh or the tear,
 The paffionate glance and foft fmile.

It

It was long ere my heart could believe,
   That a youth fo exalted as he
Would defcend to be faithful and true
   To a damfel fo humble as me :
But his words were fo open and clear,
   He would plead with fo winning a grace,
How could I but think him fincere,
   When each fentiment glow'd on his face ?

He would vow that no maiden befides
   E'er poffefs'd fuch a fhare of his heart ;
And before he'd relinquifh my love,
   With his titles and wealth he would part :
That juft was his every intent,
   That he ever moft conftant would prove ;
And tho' a proud lord by defcent,
   He would be a mean fhepherd in love :

That fimplicity, fweetnefs, and truth,
   Could only enamour his breaft ;
That in me was their union complete,
   And on me his affection fhould reft :

H

For

For the dames of the town had forfook
  Every charm that engages the heart;
That each fentiment, action, and look,
  Like their faces, were cover'd by art.

When the fcreech-owl and raven's harfh notes
  O'er the nightingale's fong fhall prevail;
When the glare of the pencil or loom
  Shall vie with the rofe of the vale;
Then the polifh'd coquette fhall compare
  With thy artlefs perfections, he cries;
Then the diamonds in CHLORIS's hair
  Shall rival my PHILLIS's eyes.

He would vow, from a heart fo fincere
  Not a moment his paffion fhould range;
He would bid me depend on his love,
  That it never fhould vary or change:
Thus he talk'd, and I fondly believ'd,
  Till gay fummer fled jocund away;
But no longer, alas! I'm deceiv'd,
  Not my tears can induce him to ftay.

3   Brown

Brown autumn, retiring apace,
 To winter refigns up the year;
How faint are the fun's chearing rays,
 How fickly does Nature appear!
The hawthorn, which late was fo gay,
 How thorny, mifhapen, and bare!
No longer the thrufh tunes his lay,
 Or the violet perfumes the fweet air.

Gay fummer, returning again,
 Shall bid the fweet violet bloom;
The hawthorn again fhall be gay,
 And the thrufh his foft note fhall refume:
But ne'er can gay fummer's return
 This ravage and ruin repair,
Or bid the fad heart ceafe to mourn
 That is blafted by love and defpair.

PASTORAL THE THIRD.

MY days in sweet mirth still returning were spent,
No shepherd was e'er more than COLIN content;
While LUCY was with me each joy did I prove,
Nor envy'd a monarch, possess'd of her love :
Each morn at my cart and my plough still I smil'd,
I valu'd no labour, for LUCY I toil'd ;
And at eve, when returning along the gay plains,
One kiss from her lips would repay all my pains.

The birds chanted music in every grove,
And the gale breath'd perfume to enliven my love ;
How gay were the woodbines that dress'd my calm cot,
How sweet was my labour, how bless'd was my lot!
But, alas ! she is gone, and away is fled joy ;
All the day do I mourn, all the night do I sigh ;
Of my cot I grow weary, neglect my poor sheep,
For now LUCY is gone I do nothing but weep.

What

What avails that my cottage with woodbines is drefs'd,

That my fields are more verdant and rich than the reft;

That all playful my heifers and lambkins appear,

That the grotto is cool, and the rivulet clear?

What avails, when I go to the wake or the fair,

That I'm reckon'd the clevereft fwain that comes there,

If Lucy, unmov'd by my merit and charms,

Defpifes my paffion, and flies from my arms?

See my pipe, how neglected, thrown carelefs away,

No longer attun'd to her favourite lay!

See the lambkin I taught to take food from her hands,

How mutely complaining, how penfive he ftands!

Ah never, falfe Lucy! (believe what I tell)

Shalt thou meet with another that loves thee fo well!

Ah never, tho' ardent and true they appear,

Shalt thou meet with a paffion fo warm and fincere!

PASTORAL THE FOURTH.

SEE, DAPHNE, see the opening morn
  Gilds every dew-drop on the thorn!
See how the sun's first trembling beam
Plays in yon riv'let's silver stream!
See how that riv'let, as it flows,
Kisses the down-bent blushing rose,
Who hangs her head, o'ercharg'd with dew,
In the clear stream her like to view!

See how yon lofty hills arise,
And seem to prop the vaulted skies!
See yon tall oaks their branches rear,
And scorn the threat'ning storm to fear!
Again behold that humbler grove,
Which zephyrs fan, and wood-nymphs love!
Behold that lawn's enamel'd green!—
All this from DAMON's cot is seen.

And

And deign, my love, to caſt thy gentle eyes
Where DAMON's humble, peaceful cottage lies:
His cot, tho' ſmall, with each convenience bleſs'd;
Tho' low the roof, with moſs and woodbines dreſs'd.
Freſh is the air, and healthful is the dale,
Blooming-the flowers, whoſe ſweets perfume the gale:
Oh! come and breathe the air, come view the ſcene,
Which from thy DAMON's peaceful cot is ſeen.

Alas! if DAPHNE be not there,
All clouded does the morn appear;
The river diſcontented flows,
Nor ſtops to kiſs the bending roſe;
All rugged yonder hills aſcend,
Rude ſtorms appear yon oaks to rend;
The grove, the lawn, no more are green,
No charm from DAMON's cot is ſeen.

The fragrant woodbine hangs its head,
Its ſweets are loſt, its beauty fled;
No more the roſe its charms can boaſt,
The air has all its freſhneſs loſt;

Lawns,

Lawns, groves, and ftreams appear to moar,

Their charms difpers'd, their fweetnefs gone.

Ah ! if my DAPHNE be not there,

How fad does DAMON's cot appear !

But come, my love ! to welcome thee

All Nature fmiles, all join with me :

Come, make thy DAMON's cottage gay,

Let all things breathe the fweets of May ;

Cull each fair flower that paints the lawn,

Our chearful dwelling to adorn.

Were DAMON's cot adorn'd by thee,

Ah ! what a cot would DAMON's be !

PASTORAL

PASTORAL THE FIFTH.

SURE happiness is but a name,
 That deceives us with fancy'd delight;
A bright, but fantastical flame,
 Which appears but to fade from the sight.
My PHILLIDA's smile was so sweet,
 And her words were so artless and kind,
That I could not suspect of deceit,
 What appear'd so sincere, so refin'd.

What merit does THIRSIS possess
 That I may not well reckon my own?
Does he woo with superior address?
 Has his pipe a more musical tone?
Tho' he trips it so light on the plain,
 As lightly my steps bound along;
As soft is my pastoral strain,
 As engaging and sweet is my song.

But

But he boasts the smooth skill to persuade,

   In flattery's mean arts he excels,

And he scorns and exposes the maid

   Who believes the false tales that he tells.

Ah! PHILLIS, believe not his tale,

   His often-chang'd passion despise!

Ah! let not his falshood prevail,

   Regard not his oaths or his sighs!

But PHILLIDA's vows are forgot,

   My fond eyes she refuses to bless;

She despises my rustical cot,

   And courts the false shepherd's addrefs.

Yet why should such trifles give pain?

   Why am I so easily mov'd?

Tho' with THIRSIS she danc'd on the plain,

   ALEXIS is not less belov'd.

When THIRSIS a garland did bring,

   And laid it at PHILLIDA's feet,

Compos'd of each flower of the spring,

   She declar'd that the roses were sweet.

Why

Why did she the present receive?

Ah! why did she smile on the swain?

Till then I could never believe

That my PHILLIDA's smile could give pain.

Yet let me not rashly complain,

My charmer still faithful may prove;

Why then does she fly from the plain?

Why does she not smile on her love?

But perhaps I offended her ears

With harsh words that were hasty and wrong;

Ah! PHILLIS, forgive the wild fears

Of a passion too ardent and strong!

Forgive the harsh things that I said;

They did not proceed from my heart:

Hadst thou seen how it inwardly bled,

Thy own would have felt for its smart.

Forgive me! and quickly appear,

My heart and my lambkins to share;

Oh! prove that thy love is sincere,

Or ALEXIS will die of despair.

PASTORAL

PASTORAL THE SIXTH.

TALK not of contentment and eafe,
 Say not grief will my beauty deftroy;
No more I'm ambitious to pleafe,
 He is gone whofe applaufe was my joy.
My love was the pride of the plains,
 With him could no fhepherd compare;
He was envy'd and fear'd by the fwains,
 But admir'd by each fenfible fair.

How fondly I lov'd the dear youth
 My fighs and my blufhes can prove;
But he never fufpected the truth,
 Ne'er imagin'd thofe blufhes were love.
How I dreaded that love fhould appear,
 When delighted I view'd every grace!
Sure each thought of his breaft was fincere,
 For each thought was imprefs'd on his face.

What

What a trembling has feiz'd my whole frame,
   Oh! how it would thrill thro' each part!
If another but mention'd his name,
   What fluttering I felt at my heart!
On his form unobferv'd when I gaz'd,
   While his eyes on fair CHLOE were turn'd,
If thofe eyes to my face he has rais'd,
   How my breaft with confufion has burn'd!

Tho' they tell me for love I was made,
   That my wit can each bofom alarm,
Yet my tongue ftill refus'd me its aid,
   When I moft was ambitious to charm.
Before I beheld the dear fwain,
   No maid was fo chearful as I;
Not a fhepherd or nymph of the plain
   E'er difcover'd me venting a figh:

Each maid did I love as a friend,
   I felt for each fair-one's diftrefs;
For beauty I ne'er would contend,
   Never wifh'd their perfections were lefs.

                       But

But now, O how alter'd am I!

How mean and ungenerous grown!

Not a charm that I fee them enjoy,

But I inftantly wifh it my own.

ALEXIS, return to the plain!

All grief, all dejection remove;

But, alas! he fufpects not my pain,

He fufpects not poor PHILLIDA's love.

With CHLOE, the rich and the fair,

Thro' fcenes of delight does he range;

Yet, ah! fimple fhepherd, beware,

For CHLOE, fair CHLOE, can change.

Tho' her eyes like the diamond appear,

Tho' her lips drink the ruby's bright hue,

Yet poor PHILLIDA's heart is fincere,

Her affection is conftant and true:

But fair CHLOE is greater thàn I,

And ambition thy foul has poffefs'd;

It has bound thee with magical tie,

And quite feal'd up the door of thy breaft.

ALEXIS

ALEXIS the cottage difdains,

    He haftes where the great-ones refort;

He will never return to the plains,

    With gay CHLOE he flies to the court.

Then no more of my griefs let me fpeak,

    Thofe griefs may ALEXIS ne'er know!

Yes, poor feeling heart, thou may'ft break,

    But ne'er fhalt difcover thy woe!

PASTORAL

PASTORAL THE SEVENTH.

HOW fweet were the days I have feen,
 (Ah me ! that fuch pleafurcs fhould fade !)
When I tended my flock on the green,
 Or reclin'd with my pipe in the fhade !
My heart was a ftranger to woe,
 It knew not ambition or fear ;
My flock was as white as the fnow,
 And my pipe than the blackbird more clear.

Undifturb'd was my nightly repofe,
 Gay dreams added pleafure to reft ;
Full of vigour and lightnefs I 1ofe,
 Ere the lark left his grafs-woven neft :
Ripe harveft embrown'd my rich field,
 With woodbines the hedges were crown'd ;
How fweet the perfume it would yield !
 How it flung its wild branches around !

How

How pleasingly summer has flown;
    Nor fear'd I cold winter so drear;
My well-cover'd cot was my own,
    And DAPHNE, dear DAPHNE, was there!
What gladness her sight would inspire!
    Her charms were the theme of my lay;
With fresh fuel I loaded my fire,
    And carol'd the evening away.

For her my clear fountain o'erflows,
    For her spread the oak and the pine;
For her pleasure I planted the rose,
    For her taste prun'd and cultur'd my vine.
To a palace, where monarchs reside,
    She prefer'd my calm humble retreat;
She envy'd no queen in her pride;
    She would smile, and my joy was compleat.

Such felicity what could destroy,
    But the absence of her I adore?
She smil'd every object to joy;
    She is gone, and they charm me no more.

I   Her

Her prefence gave fummer its bloom,

 For her the rich harveft I ftor'd :

No longer can rofes perfume,

 Nor the grape any fweetnefs afford.

But 'tis friendfhip has call'd her away ;

 How then can I her abfence reprove ?

Yet, ah ! why prolongs fhe her ftay ?

 Can cold friendfhip be dearer than love ?

I am fure fhe would hafte her return,

 Did fhe know of my anguifh and fears ;

How each moment her abfence I mourn,

 And how dull every pleafure appears.

In the dance when the villagers join,

 Crown'd with garlands and chaplets fo gay,

'Tis her abfence allows them to fhine,

 They look fair becaufe fhe is away.

Now Lucy the vain is admir'd,

 Now Chloe and Delia delight ;

When the monarch of day is retir'd,

 We adore the pale regent of night.

In

In the dance when the villagers join,

   Crown'd with garlands and chaplets fo gay,

While I gaze how I inly repine,

   And accufe my lov'd charmer's delay.

But why thus fhould I figh and complain?

   I will follow the fteps of my love;

I will bring her again to the plain,

   And her prefence all care fhall remove.

Then her charms fhall enliven my fong,

   To my pipe fhall foft echo refound;

By her fide the fweet theme I'll prolong,

   And the blackbird fhall mimic the found:

My cot fhall be chearful again,

   She fhall blefs my calm humble retreat;

Again fhall fhe fmile on her fwain,

   And his joy fhall again be complete.

PASTORAL THE EIGHTH.

SEE how the sweet eglantines mourn !
 See the roses with blushes declare,
That they bloom'd for ALEXIS alone,
 That they fade when the shepherd's not here !

Approach, ye sad virgins, and say,
 Did ye ever behold such a youth ?
He was mild and engaging as May,
 He was open and fearless as truth.

He never a worm would annoy,
 Yet the high-mettled steed could controul ;
He dar'd not an insect destroy,
 Yet he shrunk not when thunder did roll.

When he tun'd the sweet pastoral lays,
 How the shepherds around him would throng !
How the air would resound with his praise !
 How they sigh'd when he finish'd his song !

5   Ah

Ah me! 'twas fo gentle and fweet!

 He would play with fuch foftnefs and art,

That the founds in my bofom would beat,

 For the mufic funk into my heart.

My fhepherd to me was fo dear,

 That my heart ne'er again fhall know peace:

Ye virgins, my love was fincere,

 My affection can never decreafe.

With his lofs my continual theme,

 Thro' the vallies and woodlands I'll rove;

With my tears I'll augment the dull ftream,

 And fad Echo fhall figh for my love.

Ah! vainly our lofs we deplore!

 In vain do we figh and complain!

Can our forrows ALEXIS reftore,

 Or give PHILLIDA eafe from her pain?

Yet ftill, while remembrance fhall laft,

 While merit and virtue fhall move,

I'll hang o'er the joys that are paft,

 Still reflect on his truth and his love.

Then

Then away with the pipe and the fong;

 Come, virgins, with me to deplore:

Let fighs be the notes we prolong,

 For ALEXIS, our pride, is no more!

INSCRIPTION

FOR A SEQUESTERED RETREAT, CALLED THE BOWER

OF OBERON,

IN A BEAUTIFUL ROMANTIC PLEASURE-GROUND.

ROUND thefe fair fcenes direct your eyes,
　　Nor let their beauties raife furprize ;
The various wonders that ye fee
(Be grateful, mortals) fpring from me.
O'er this enchanted vale I reign,
And here my elfin ftate maintain :
On me the fairy race depend,
A thoufand fprites my nod attend ;
Beneath each fhining leaf they lie,
Unfeen by grofs material eye ;
With charms each bending branch is bound,
And many a magic fpell is round.
　　Tremble, thou wretch, whofe fordid breaft
By felfifh paffions is poffefs'd !

　　　　　Whofe

Whofe foul is mean and infincere;

Tremble, nor dare to enter here!

Expos'd thy every thought fhall lie,

Thy heart be read by every eye.

But let the generous, brave, and kind,

The foul fincere, the cultur'd mind,

Unaw'd by guilt-purfuing fear,

And freely welcome, enter here.

    For fuch I fcatter fweets around,

And deck this fair enchanted ground;

For fuch this clofe retreat I made,

For fuch I rais'd this magic fhade;

Their fteps with guardian care I guide,

And turn each danger far afide;

The evening damps I waft away,

And fan with frefh'ning gales the day;

With brighter glow I gild the morn,

I hang the dew-drops on the thorn;

The fwelling bud I watchful tend,

From worms and chilling blights defend;

I give its tints a livelier bloom,

And bid it breathe more rich perfume;

                              I polifh

I polifh yon tranfparent lake,

I drefs with rofes yonder brake;

The lofty mountain I illume,

And give the dell its folemn gloom;

I make the bubbling fountain fpring,

I teach the linnet how to fing.

 Come then, ye juftly favour'd few,

Thefe beauteous fcenes were form'd for you.

Repofe ye in my fairy bowers,

And tafte the ftream, and prefs the flowers;

Gay dreams, by livelieft fancy drefs'd,

Shall hover round ye while ye reft.

Come then, unaw'd by guilty fear,

And, freely welcome, enter here.

INSCRIPTION,

INSCRIPTION,

TO BE HUNG UPON A LARGE OLD TREE,

WHICH STANDS OPPOSITE A ROCK, THAT

OCCASIONS A STRONG ECHO.

OH! ye who haunt this peaceful vale,
 Beware what themes ye make your choice;
Dare not a guilty wish reveal,
 Left ye're betray'd by Echo's voice.

For there, in yonder pine-crown'd rock,
 Midft many a winding cave she dwells,
Catching each faintly-paffing found,
 Which to the winds aloud she tells.

Let not the guiltlefs bofom fear,
 Each virtuous theme will be its choice;
Nought hurtful to the good dwells here,
 Innocence fears not Echo's voice.

INSCRIPTION

INSCRIPTION

FOR THE ENTRANCE OF A SOLITARY WALK, LEADING
TO A HERMITAGE;

HUNG UPON A TREE WITH A SEAT UNDER IT.

STRANGER, would'ft thou enter here,
 Leave behind thee guilty Fear;
Root Ambition from thy mind,
Give Care and Envy to the wind:
No fuch paffions fhould intrude
On the fweets of folitude.

Bring varying Fancy, ever young;
Bring Judgment clear, and Reafon ftrong;
Bring chearful Hope, fair Virtue's child;
Bring lowly Temperance, chafte and mild;
Bring Contemplation, filent maid,
Who loves to haunt the folemn fhade.

With

With thefe, if Philofophic Eafe,

If pure Simplicity can pleafe,

Here, ftranger, reft, or freely rove

O'er yon rock, or thro' yon grove,

Secure ;—no ill can e'er intrude

On Virtue and fweet Solitude.

FOR THE ENTRANCE OF THE HERMITAGE.

I F, by Contemplation led,

 And love of Wifdom's facred lore,

The lowly vale thy fteps would tread,

 Or trace the upland thicket o'er,

Awhile repofe thee in my cell,

Where Contemplation loves to dwell.

Oft-times does the courtly fair

 Deign to vifit my retreat,

Quitting the world's fantaftic glare

 For fober thought and converfe fweet ;

Then fcorn not thou the lowly cell,

Where Grace and Beauty love to dwell.

If

If cruel cares difturb thy breaft,
 And rob thy troubled foul of peace,
Enter here, fecure of reft,
 And bid each ruder paffion ceafe ;
No cruel cares difturb the cell,
Where Truth and Wifdom love to dwell.

Let not folitude alarm,
 Or fill thy timid breaft with fear ;
To guard this facred fpot from harm
 Friendly fprites unfeen are near ;
Nought hurtful can approach the cell,
Where Peace and Virtue love to dwell.

TO BE PLACED WITHIN THE HERMITAGE,

COME, Nature's children, ye who love, like me,
The peaceful dwellings of Simplicity,
Who court the woodland folitude, and know
The fweets that from divine reflection flow ;
Come, fhare the counfels of my aged breaft,
Come, tafte with me the fweets of rural reft.

And

And ye, whom meaner joys can more invite,

Whom feaft and fong, and midnight dance delight,

Ah! paufe awhile 'midft pleafure's wild career,

The voice of reafon, of experience, hear.

Believe not all is joy that boafts the name;

Believe not pleafure and excefs the fame:

Difguft and difappointment ftill await

The numerous wifhes luxuries create;

While he who little wants, can greatly rife

Above their pleafures, and their pains defpife.

When fmiles the fpring, and every vernal hour

Gives birth to fome frefh herb or painted flower,

From yonder mead my fweet repaft I bring,

And draw my bev'rage from yon healthful fpring:

When winter bites, the frugal fquirrel's hoard

Of cluft'ring filberts crowns my fimple board;

Dry'd leaves and rufhes form my artlefs bed,

And fragrant mofs fupports my carelefs head;

No tyrant paffions rule my peaceful breaft,

No hoarded treafures break my needful reft.

Learn hence how few are Nature's wants, and treat

With juft contempt the vainly rich and great;

Let

Let not thy cares, to vulgar fenfe confin'd,

Leave bare and unimprov'd th' immortal mind;

Read Nature's ever new and open page,

Till higher views thy rifing foul engage:

Fair Solitude thy weak refolves fhall aid,

To Wifdom's bright abode thy fteps fhall lead:

Her paths, when trac'd with care, are fmooth and plain;

Never was heavenly Wifdom fought in vain.

WRITTEN

WRITTEN EXTEMPORE,

UPON SEEING AN ELEGANT DAIRY-HOUSE ERECTED
UPON THE SPOT WHERE A DOG-KENNEL HAD
FORMERLY STOOD, IN THE PARK AT WYNSTAY,
THE SEAT OF SIR W. W. W. BART.

THE morning was frefh, the fweet air was perfum'd,
 With the funfhine of May was each object illum'd;
The leaves glitter'd bright with a foft-falling fhower,
And the drops flood impearl'd on each thorn and each
  flower;
When COLIN met THIRSIS, the friend of his youth,
Whom he lov'd and efteem'd for his fenfe and his truth:
The ready-ftretch'd hand they alternately prefs'd,
And with friendly enquiries each other addrefs'd.
The how-d'ye-do's over, cries COLIN, How fweet
Is each fcene in thefe grounds, and the whole how
  complete;

            Fair

Fair Nature, luxuriant, enlivens each part,

Refin'd and corrected, not fetter'd by Art :

Yet some alteration appears to my eye;

'Tis some way improv'd, yet I cannot tell why.

Quoth THIRSIS, and smil'd, My good friend, thou
    art right;

The improvement affects both the heart and the sight:

For it shows, what ten thousand bright actions have
   shown,

True taste and true goodness united in one.

On that spot, now so fair, in despite of all taste,

A cumberous load of rude building was plac'd,

Within the inclosure of whose ample bound

Perpetually howl'd the dissatisfy'd hound;

Their dissonance fill'd the calm groves with dismay,

And affrighted the sylvans and wood-nymphs away.

No longer the thrush his soft note could prolong,

Nor the lark, till half mounted, durst warble his song.

The Muses, who wont in the valley to rove,

To sport on the hill, or repose in the grove,

All scar'd by the sound, in a hurry and fright,

To Stow, and the Leasowes, and Hagley, took flight;

        Their

Their cry, and the harſh piercing notes of the horn,
Inſtead of the wood-lark, awaken'd the morn:
The ſwains gaze amaz'd, then, with boiſterous ſhout,
Quit the plough and the ſonnet to follow the rout;
From rock, mountain, and valley loud tumults ariſe,
While Echo joins concert, and doubles the cries.

  Thus confuſion reign'd wide, till the lord of the ſoil
Beheld how the peaſant was lur'd from his toil;
Beheld (for to him, by the favour of Heaven,
Taſte, genius, diſcernment, and goodneſs were given)
How, beſtow'd on a noiſy irregular train,
His bounty perverted, was laviſh'd in vain.
In his mind, quick conceiving, the generous thought
No ſooner had birth than to action 'twas brought;
And what Ovid, that fabling poet of old,
Of the cot of Philemon and Baucis has told,
How where whilom it ſtood was a temple erected.
Fy the magical power of his word was effected
The diſſonance ceas'd which offended the ear;
The cumberous building, the hounds diſappear;
Yon fair ſtructure aroſe to adorn the gay plains,
Where elegance ſmiles, and ſimplicity reigns.

No

No longer the ſhrill piercing notes of the horn

Break the ſhepherd's repoſe ere the lark wakes the morn;

Inſtead of the huntſman with boiſterous throng,

The neat-looking dairy-maid trips it along:

Salubrious ſtreams fill her ſnow-colour'd pail,

Whoſe approach from a diſtance the cottagers hail;

Delighted they quaff the ſweet beverage of health,

While they bleſs their kind patron, and pray for his
   wealth.

Now gently ſoft echo reſounds thro' the vale,

To the pipe of the ſhepherd, and love's ſoothing tale;

Inſtead of fierce howls, and each diſſonant ſound,

Flocks bleat from the mountains, and herds low around;

The wood-nymphs again dance the thickets among,

And the lark and the thruſh undiſturb'd tune their ſong;

The Muſes no longer are frighted away,

But have fix'd, with the Virtues, their home at Wynſtay.

F I N I S.

9 781115 965156